# on the train

Carron Brown

Illustrated by Bee Johnson

IVY KIDS

# A railway depot is bustling with activity.

If you peer between the engines in
the sheds, through the carriages and
down the platforms, you can
see different kinds of trains.

Shine a torch behind the page,
or hold it up to the light to spot
drivers, engineers, passengers
and freight. Discover a world
of great surprises.

Before they travel, the trains are checked and tested by engineers.

Can you see what happens in the blue shed?

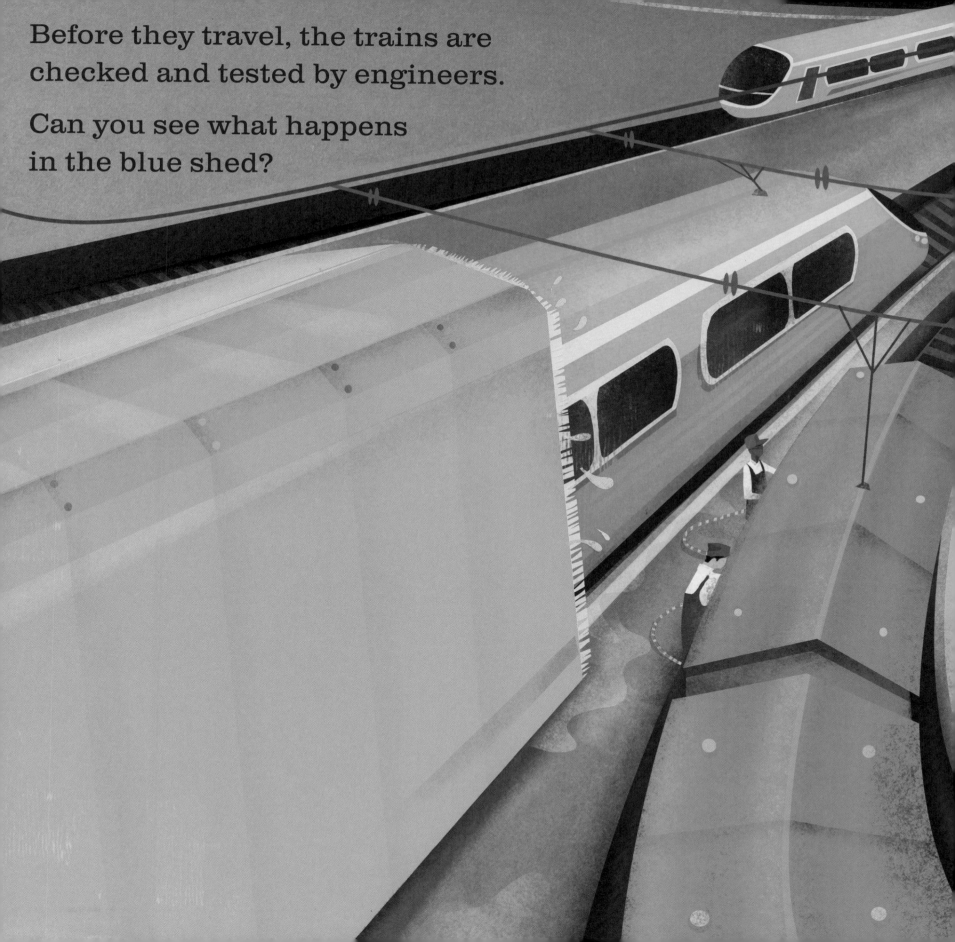

This engine is moving
through a train wash.

Spinning rollers cover
it in soap and water
to make it sparkle.

Swish!

Swish!

Splish!

This train's windows are cleaned before its next journey.

Can you see another engineer at work?

# Glug! Glug!

This train runs on fuel called diesel.

The engineer connects the fuel pump to the train and fills the tank with diesel.

# All aboard!

The guard on the platform is blowing his whistle to let the driver know it's safe to go.

Who is checking the tickets?

# Click! Clack!

The conductor checks each ticket, then punches a hole in it.

Passengers can ask the conductor questions about the journey.

The doors close and our train moves out of the station.

Take a peek inside
the driver's cab.

# Whoosh!

The driver pushes on
the speed control.

This makes the train
travel faster – around
160 kilometres per hour.

Rumble!
Rumble!

Our train stops
at a red signal.

A goods train rolls by.
Can you see what's
inside the trucks?

# Brrrr!

These containers are cold to keep
food fresh. There are onions from
a farm and fish from the sea.

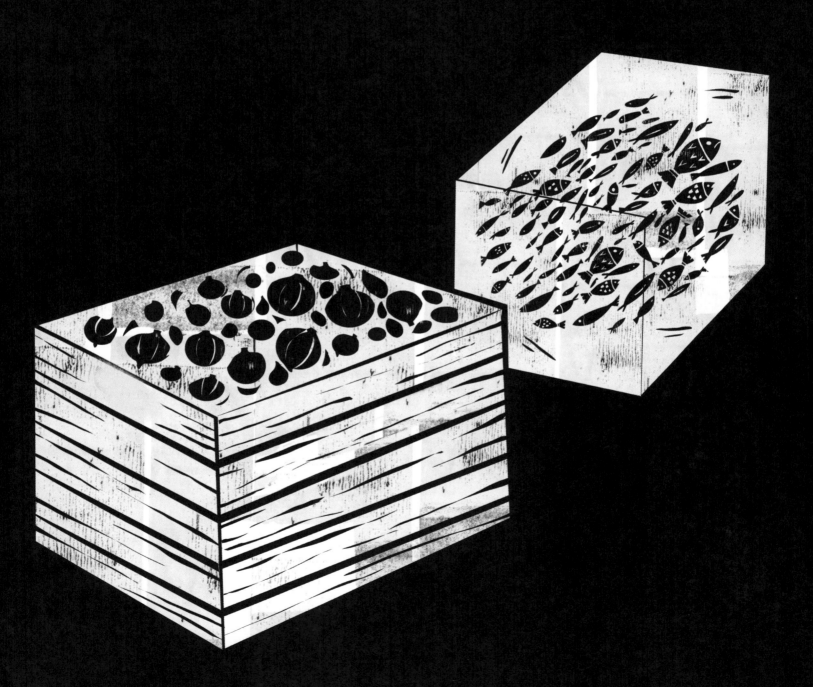

Look out the window. Behind the hill,
smoke billows from a faraway train.

What kind
of train
makes smoke?

A steam engine high up on a viaduct.

Pufff!

Pufff!

A viaduct is a long, high bridge that crosses over a valley or a river.

The engine burns coal to make
steam. Let's peek inside...

# Weeesh!

The steam rushes out of the boiler
and pushes the pistons that turn
the engine's wheels.

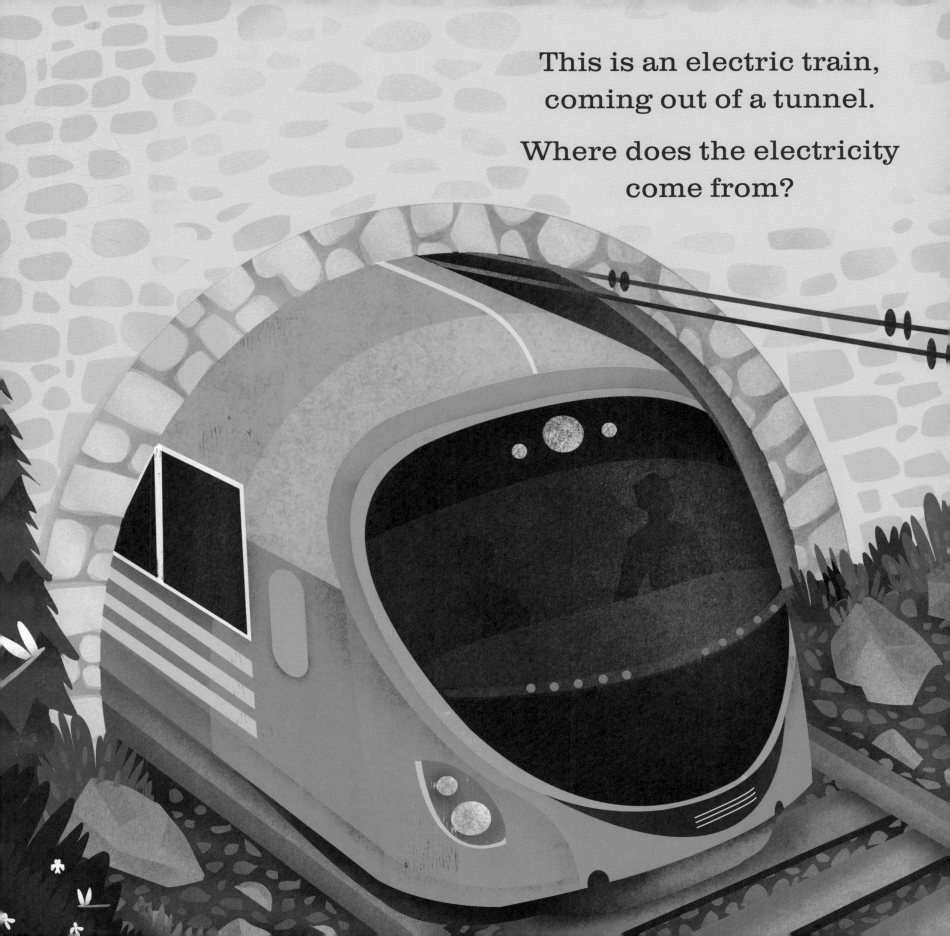

This is an electric train,
coming out of a tunnel.

Where does the electricity
come from?

Zzzzip!

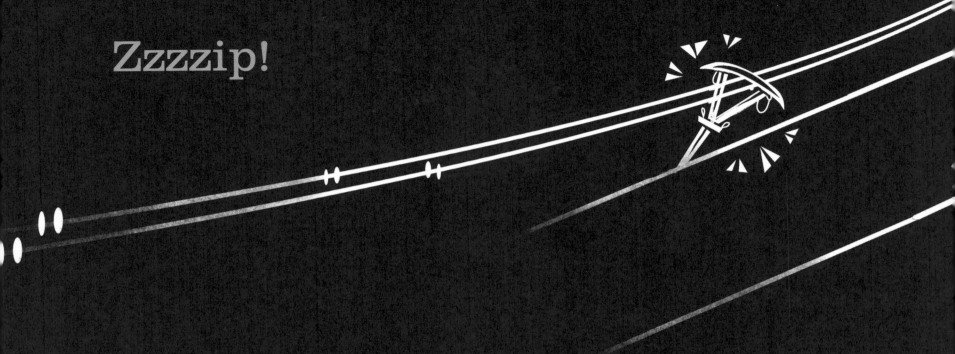

Crackle!

A metal rod, called a pantograph, reaches
up and slides along overhead wires.

Electricity runs down the
pantograph to power the train.

Our train is changing direction.

Can you see why?

Engineers wearing hard hats
are fixing the rails.

A machine helps them lay new
tracks in the right place.

Clank!

Clank!

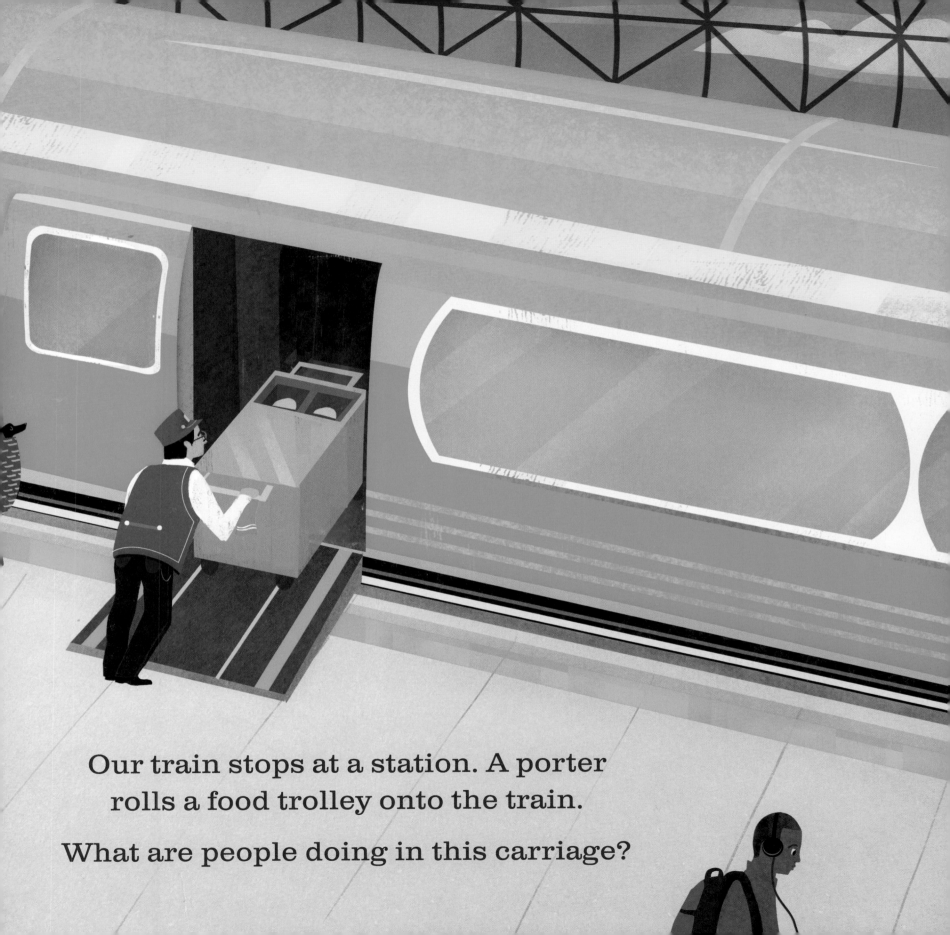

Our train stops at a station. A porter rolls a food trolley onto the train.

What are people doing in this carriage?

# Eating!

This is the buffet carriage. Here passengers
sit down for a meal or a drink.

The green train has stopped to let the passenger train pass by.

What are people doing in the white train?

Sleeping...

# Ssshhhh!

Passengers sleep in cabins with beds.
The train travels through the night.

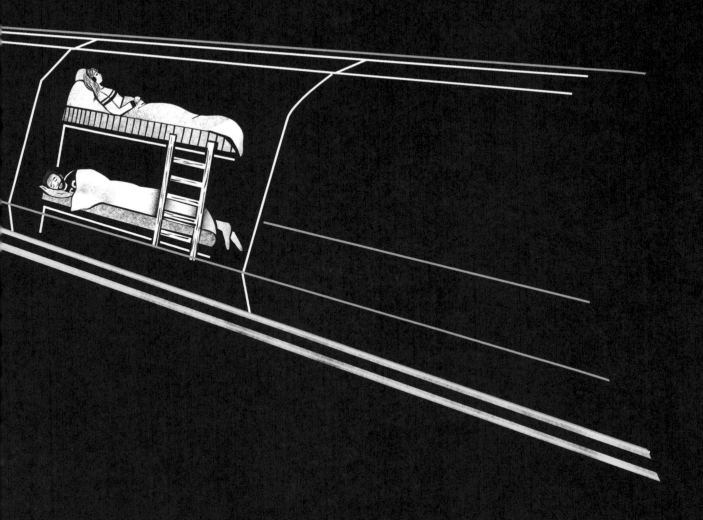

# Honk! Honk!

A train sounds its horn as
it travels through a town.

What's on the other
side of the track?

Cars and people wait by a level crossing.

Vroom!
Vroom!

The barrier will rise
when it is safe to cross.

The guard on our train announces the last stop.
People stand up and get ready to leave.

What's inside their luggage?

# Mee-ow!

Some pets can travel on trains, too.
Cats go in special carriers.

Our train arrives in the city. We will get off this train and travel on an underground train, instead...

# Clickety-clack!

Underground trains run under
the city through long tunnels.

It's a fast way to travel from
one part of town to another.

Our train uses its brakes to
stop in the station.

What else can stop the train?

Buffers help to stop the train.
They show the end of the line.

Our journey is over.
We have to leave our train.

Soon it will be time to
travel again. All aboard!

# There's more...

When you are at a station or inside a carriage near a window, see how many types of trains you can spot.

**Passenger trains** Fast trains carry people from one place to another. A conductor checks tickets and looks after passengers onboard. In some countries, there are double-decker carriages, with seats on two levels.

**Goods trains** have containers full of freight. Look out for different containers, such as an open-top truck for coal, a tanker for petrol and a flat-bed truck for logs. Some goods trains can be several kilometres long.

**Underground trains** Some cities have an underground railway that takes people from one place in the city to another through tunnels. Each city has a special railway map with all the stations marked.

**Maglevs** Magnetic levitation (maglev) trains hover and glide above a track. They are held in place by strong magnets. The maglev trains in Shanghai, China, are the fastest in the world. They can reach 500 kilometres per hour (310 miles per hour).